THE GREAT PHILOSOPHERS

Consulting Editors
Ray Monk and Frederic Raphael

VOLTAIRE

John Gray

ROUTLEDGE
New York

Published in 1999 by
Routledge
29 West 35th Street
New York, NY 10001

First published in 1997 by
Phoenix
A Division of the Orion Publishing Group Ltd.
Orion House
5 Upper Saint Martin's Lane
London WC2H 9F ^

Copyright © 1999 by john Gray.
Printed in the United States of America on acid-free paper.

10 9 8 7 6 5 4 3 2 1

Library of Congress Cataloging-in-Publication Data

Gray, John, 1948–
        Voltaire / John Gray.
            p. cm.—(The great philosophers : 19)
        Includes bibliographical references.
        ISBN 0-415-92394-8 (pbk.)
        1. Voltaire, 1694–1778. I. Title. II. Series: Great
        Philosophers (Routledge (Firm)) : 19.
B2177.G73 1999
194—dc21   99-20651
                                                        CIP

For Mieko

VOLTAIRE

Voltaire and Enlightenment

VOLTAIRE AND THE THEODICY OF THE ENLIGHTENMENT

Voltaire is the central figure of the Enlightenment
Isaiah Berlin[1]

If, despite its history, we think of philosophy as the disinterested pursuit of truth, then Voltaire was no philosopher. He lived and died, the exemplary *philosophe*, a partisan. Nothing is further from Voltaire's thought than the spirit of inquiry. Nor, despite his excoriating sarcasm and the unquenchable vivacity of his pessimism, was Voltaire's view of humankind detached or cynical. He was a lifelong propagandist for a secular faith. The object of Voltaire's 'philosophy' was not to advance inquiry, still less to foster sceptical doubt. It was to found a new creed. Voltaire sought to supplant the Christian religion by the humanist faith of the Enlightenment. His tireless raillery was meant in deadly earnest. His opposition to Christian fanaticism had itself a fanatical bent. Voltaire's life's work was to set European life on a new foundation by constructing a successor to Christianity.

Voltaire's mockery of Christian superstitions and enthusiasms Christian served a new religion of universal enlightenment. But his Enlightenment creed did not make as radical a break with Christianity as he and the other *philosophes* liked to believe. It inherited a good deal from the religion he meant it to supplant. The Enlightenment shared with Christianity vast hopes for the emancipation of humankind – and deep intolerance towards anything that stood in the way of their universal ambitions. It is because they have so much in common that Christians and believers in Enlightenment have always been such intimate enemies. Among their common dispositions is a suspicion of any kind of intellectual inquiry whose upshot is not sanctioned by morality.

For Voltaire, philosophy was not an intellectual adventure whose end is always in doubt. Like the natural sciences, which he believed it would come increasingly to resemble, philosophy was an instrument of human emancipation. Voltaire had no doubts about what that emancipation consisted in. Bleak as was his view of the history of the species, and uncertain though he judged its prospects to be, what human emancipation *means* is, for Voltaire and his posterity, remarkably – even incredibly – unproblematic. Freedom from superstition, the growth of wealth and knowledge, progress towards a universal civilization – this Enlightenment project, never questioned, animated Voltaire throughout his adult life. It inspired his tireless campaigns against injustice and his unending ridicule of the authorities of his age.

Voltaire never subjected the beliefs and values that animated the Enlightenment to any extended investigation. To be sure, he was only too aware of the difficulties that stood in the way of the universal, rational civilization he and the other *philosophes* favoured. Indeed, he was inclined to regard civilization itself as an intermittent episode in the natural history of barbarism. But he was too preoccupied with the struggles of the day to question the ideal he served all his life. He did not ask whether much that is worthwhile might be lost in the world to which he aspired. Nor did he explore the conflicts that might arise among the values that would be central in such a world. He lacked the inclination, and indeed the time, to ask questions whose answers might not serve the cause to which he was indefatigably committed. It was, after all, the cause – as he saw it – of humanity.

Partly for these reasons, Voltaire's writings on philosophical questions are unoriginal to the last degree. They amount to little more than a reworking of some ideas from John Locke and Pierre Bayle. Few of the entries in his *Philosophical Dictionary* are concerned with philosophical questions. Voltaire made no contribution to moral philosophy or to the theory of knowledge. Unlike Hume, or even Adam Smith, he did not leave an inheritance on which generations of later philosophers were to draw. If Voltaire can be said to have had a 'philosophy', it has today only a historical interest.

Yet, as Nietzsche intimated when he identified him as one of his few predecessors, Voltaire's thought has a profound and enduring interest. More clearly than any other European thinker, he exemplifies and illuminates the limitations and contradictions of the Enlightenment – that extended family of intellectual and political movements, highly disparate and sometimes falling out among themselves, which flourished in several European countries – notably France, Scotland and Germany – in the eighteenth century, and which shapes much of our thinking today. Unlike his derivative and dated 'philosophy', Voltaire's contribution to our understanding of the Enlightenment and thereby to European thought remains indispensable today.

The Enlightenment cannot be understood except in the context of the creed that it aimed to supplant. Though this was most marked in Catholic countries, the *philosophes* were everywhere enemies of Christianity. But their ideals and beliefs were marked indelibly by the religion they sought to extirpate. They were in love with the world before the advent of Christianity (as they imagined it to have been); but even the most complete pagans among them, such as Voltaire himself, were able to enter into a post-Christian view of things only very incompletely. They were themselves too moved by the stupendous moral hopes that Christianity had kindled ever to leave it altogether behind. In consequence, they were never able to emancipate themselves fully from the faith they spent their lives condemning.

At times Voltaire's hatred of Christianity led him into bigotry. His anti-Semitism originated partly in his hatred of Christianity. Like his great admirer, Nietzsche, he could not forgive the people that had given birth to Christianity. At the same time Voltaire's repellent anti-Semitic prejudices were merely those of all of European Christendom. They show how incomplete was his emancipation from that now vanished world. Like Nietzsche's, Voltaire's recurrent fascination with 'the sublime misanthropist' Pascal was evidence of a repressed affinity as much as of an avowed enmity.

'To admire Voltaire', wrote Joseph de Maistre, ultra-reactionary, Catholic, doyen of the Counter-Enlightenment and one of Voltaire's most formidable opponents, 'is the sign of a corrupt heart, and if anyone is drawn to his works, then be sure that God does not love him.' In his *Soirées de St Petersburg*, the great reactionary thinker describes Voltaire as the most dangerous of all the *philosophes*, since he 'employed the greatest talent with most coolness to do most mischief'. De Maistre's view of Voltaire as a scoffing subverter of religion was echoed by William Blake, when he wrote in his *Notebook*

> Mock on Mock on Voltaire Rousseau
> Mock on Mock on tis all in vain

4

> You throw the sand against the wind
> And the wind throws it back again[2]

Yet, though he declared that 'Every honourable man must view the Christian sect with horror', and anathematized the Christian religion with the celebrated formula *Ecrasez l'infâme! Crush the infamy!* (a formula sometimes prudently abbreviated in his notebooks and correspondence to *Ecr. l'inf.*), Voltaire was never an atheist.

In an early poem, Voltaire wrote that he was not a Christian in order that he might love God better. After an early morning walk with a visitor to his beautiful retreat in Ferney, Voltaire surveyed the panoramic view and – in all sincerity, it seems – proclaimed: 'All-powerful God! I believe!' And, as if to fend off any impression that his hostility to Christianity might have abated, he went on: 'As for Monsieur the Son and Madame His Mother, that's another story.'

Throughout his long life Voltaire's sharp tongue and acrid wit belied his seriousness of intent. Born in Paris 1694, second son of a well-to-do notary, educated at a Jesuit college, Voltaire died in 1778, only eleven years before the fall of the Bastille. A passionate valetudinarian, born weak and not expected to live, famously skeletal in his long old age, Voltaire survived three French monarchs. He suffered from most of the diseases of his time – gout, herpes, scurvy and dropsy, to name only a few of his ailments – and often believed his last days were upon him. The unvarying regime of hard work he imposed upon himself may have arisen from the sense of having a short life that he carried with him from a sickly, possibly tubercular, childhood, as much as from the value he attached to it as an antidote to the melancholy that sometimes assailed him.

First and last Voltaire was a writer. For him writing was

not so much the expression of his thought as an instrument of self-assertion in the world. Voltaire spurned the respectable profession his father had planned for him as a lawyer for the risky career of a man who lived by his pen and his wits. He wrote without stop, devoting to writing even the time he was imprisoned in the Bastille in 1717 on suspicion of being the author of a scurrilous pamphlet, and publishing an enormous *oeuvre* during his lifetime. He did not confine himself to any one genre. He wrote plays, epic verse, philosophical tales (*contes philosophiques*), over twenty thousand letters, and essays and pamphlets almost beyond number.

Nearly everything that Voltaire wrote is unreadable today. None of his histories have entered Europe's cultural memory. Their preoccupations are too topical, their spirit too much that of his time, their style too propagandistic and their tone too unvarying in its monotonous mockery of Christianity. Voltaire's *Charles XII*, *Louis XIV* or *Annals of the Empire* do not have the enduring value of Gibbon's *Fall of the Roman Empire* or Hume's *History of England*. Though artful and sometimes brilliant, Voltaire's poems and plays read drearily now. Compared with the works of Homer and Virgil when it appeared, and establishing not only Voltaire's reputation but also the beginnings of his considerable fortune, his epic poem *La Henriade* seems irrecoverably dated to a late twentieth-century reader.

The same stilted style marks the fifty or so tragic dramas Voltaire wrote. Skilfully manufactured to suit the educated sensibility of his time, Voltaire's plays were too coldly contrived to survive the change in European taste that came with the Romantic movement. This may have been a development that Voltaire anticipated, for in the entry on 'Singing' in the *Philosophical Dictionary* he noted: 'Tragedy is now played drily; if we were not heated by the pathos of the spectacle and the action it would be very insipid. Our age, commendable in other things, is the age of dryness.'[3] It is not as a dramatist or a versifier that Voltaire is remembered.

Of all Voltaire's voluminous *oeuvre*, it is only the *contes philosophiques* that can still be read without hard and unrewarding effort. Nor is this surprising, since it is these tales that contain the essence of Voltaire as a writer and a man. In different ways the best of them are all concerned with theodicy – with the age-old struggle of humankind to reconcile itself to the evils of its condition. Of these, *Candide* is the best known as well as the best. But there is also *Micromégas*, a Swiftian satire in which human pretensions are viewed from a chilly perspective of interplanetary detachment, and *Zadig*, an ingenious 'tale of the Orient' that addresses explicitly but inconclusively the fundamental question of theodicy: Is there some design in human affairs, or must we conclude that – as Peter Reading has put it – 'men are ruled by a random Weird'?[4]

Zadig reflects on the contrast between the sublimity of the order of nature and the chaos of human life when he has to flee his native Babylon and his beloved Astarte for Egypt:

> Zadig steered his course by the stars. The constellation of Orion and the bright star of Sirius guided him, with the help of Canopus, southwards. He stared in wonder at these vast globes of light which seem to us mere feeble sparks, while the earth, which is in reality but an imperceptible point in the scheme of things, appears to our covetous eyes something so noble and grand. He saw men for what they really are, insects devouring each other upon a tiny speck of dirt. This telling image seemed to blot out his misfortunes by reminding him of

the nullity of his own being and that of Babylon. His soul soared up into the infinite and, unencumbered by his senses, beheld the immutable order of the universe. But when afterwards he considered, on coming down to earth again and reflecting once again upon his own heart, that Astarte was perhaps dead on his account, the universe ceased to exist in his eyes, and he could see nothing in the whole of nature but a dying Astarte and a hapless Zadig.[5]

Voltaire's life can be viewed as a successful experiment in self-assertion; but his own good fortune did not prevent him returning again and again to Zadig's question.

Voltaire was fully conscious of the advantages of money and from early manhood he dedicated himself to acquiring it. By the early 1720s he had become seriously rich, partly from the proceeds of his writings, but mostly through a variety of daring, occasionally shady speculative ventures. Always avaricious but rarely ungenerous, often casually charitable, Voltaire used his darting intelligence to found a great fortune. He died not only the personification of his age but a man of prodigious wealth.

The high estimation in which Voltaire held money has often evoked criticism. Yet, if the means he adopted to acquire it were sometimes dubious, his uses of it were admirable. Voltaire employed the wealth that he had amassed to ensure his independence of judgement and action, and it formed the ground of security from which he was able to challenge injustices done to those weaker than himself. Without the freedom his wealth gave him, it is doubtful that Voltaire could have launched his justly celebrated campaigns on behalf of Jean Calas and other victims of injustice.

'Voltaire' is not the name the *philosophe* was born with,

François-Marie Arouet, and its derivation remains obscure. Some have suggested that it was an abbreviation of a school nickname, 'Le Volontaire' (Master Wilful), but more likely it was an imperfect anagram of Arouet Le Jeune, Arouet the Younger. Whatever its derivation, he adopted the name in 1718, not long after his release from eleven months of imprisonment, prefixing it with an aristocratic 'de' to which nothing in his background entitled him. Voltaire's self-esteem was uncompromising. Born a bourgeois in an aristocratic age, it was inevitable that he should demand that others accept him as the nobleman he believed himself to be. Hence the title by which he came soon to be known: M. Arouet de Voltaire. Since 'Voltaire' did not exist, François-Marie Arouet found it necessary to invent him.

In 1726, after another brief spell in the Bastille occasioned by his challenging a nobleman to a duel, Voltaire departed for three years in England. There his contacts with Bolingbroke, Swift and Pope reinforced his admiration for the English and what he believed to be their tolerant, empirical outlook. He was an habitué of the French Court, enjoying for a time the favour of Madame de Pompadour, and from 1750 to 1753 he joined the court of Frederick the Great of Prussia.

Voltaire's intellectual dalliance with Frederick was ill-starred. Voltaire and Frederick had a good deal – indeed, too much – in common. They shared a bracing contempt for Christianity and the mass of humankind and an unwavering certainty that they were immune to the follies of the rest of the species. Their friendship flourished only so long as each could use the other as a mirror for his vanity.

Voltaire could never settle down as a placid, grateful pensioner, even one in the service of Europe's most enlightened monarch. Calculation, boldness and irrepressible mischief were always mixed unstably in his nature.

His instinctive need to be his own man was too strong for him to serve anyone for long. Accordingly, through a combination of his murky financial dealings and satirical pamphlets, notably his *Diatribe du Docteur Akakia*, in which he mocked the president of Frederick's Academy of Sciences, Voltaire provoked Frederick to send him away in farcical circumstances. His departure from Prussia began the last epoch of his life, which he spent in prolific and campaigning retirement in the Château de Ferney near Geneva.

Voltaire celebrated human reason, but he was not incapable of strong emotional attachments. Amongst his many romantic encounters, that with Madame du Châtelet showed Voltaire to be a delicate and devoted lover. His years with her define the epoch of his life at Cirey, where from 1734 to 1744 he lived for most of the time in a triangular *ménage* with Madame du Châtelet and her self-effacing husband, the Marquise du Châtelet.

A strong-willed and highly intelligent woman twelve years younger than Voltaire, Mme du Châtelet was not always faithful to him. The strength and depth of Voltaire's feeling for her can be judged by the immaculate courtesy with which, after an initial violent scene, he handled his lover's most serious and final infidelity with a young officer and poet, Saint-Lambert. It was shown again when Mme du Châtelet became pregnant by Saint-Lambert, safely gave birth to a child, and died a few days later. Voltaire was, for a while, inconsolable. (His mortification was aggravated by his discovery that his beloved had replaced his portrait in a ring he had given her with that of Saint-Lambert.) Mme du Châtelet's death may have been the catalyst for Voltaire's entanglement with Frederick of Prussia. At a deeper level it was the beginning of his retirement to Ferney, where he 'cultivated his garden' and orchestrated his campaigns against injustice. When he died in 1778 it was the end of an age.

Voltaire remains indispensable to European thought because in understanding him we understand something of ourselves. In the two centuries after Voltaire's death the hopes and ideals of the Enlightenment came to pervade European life. The moral and political outlook that the Enlightenment bequeathed to late modern Europe was hopeful, indeed optimistic. Its legacy to the nineteenth and twentieth centuries was a view of human history seen in terms of progress – fitful, sometimes set back by lengthy periods of barbarism, no doubt, but in the long run practically irresistible – towards a universal, rational civilization.

Along with some other eighteenth-century Enlightenment thinkers, Voltaire did not altogether share this optimistic view. Like Hume, he was often closer to such Renaissance thinkers as Machiavelli. The infamous author of *The Prince* saw history as a cycle of civilization and barbarism. He could not conceive that progress would ever cure the inherent weaknesses of civilized life, or overcome its innate propensity to relapse into barbarism. The most that could he hoped for was that skilful and illusionless leaders could prolong the life of free peoples a little beyond its natural span.

Voltaire was more hopeful than Machiavelli. But unlike much of the party of humanity he did not often allow his hopes to deform his understanding. He imagined that universal education could temper the natural stupidity and savagery of the species. Yes, by comparison with most of the Enlightenment thinkers who came after him, Voltaire's view of humankind's history and future was remarkably undeceived. His ideal of civilization was little different from that of Condorcet, Diderot, Tom Paine and Jeremy Bentham. In its most central and fundamental respects, it was shared by Marx, J.S. Mill, Spencer, Popper, Hayek, Habermas and Dewey. Voltaire shared the expectation of his age that the growth of knowledge would render human beings less savage in their treatment of their own and other species. Without this improbable and perhaps groundless hope he could not have gone on.

Yet at times Voltaire allowed himself to suspect that the horizons of human progress would always be low and clouded. At such times he gave vent to Machiavellian historical pessimism in the starkest terms. In the section of the *Philosophical Dictionary* devoted to 'Miracles' he wrote: 'After raising itself for a time from one bog, the world falls back into another; an age of barbarism follows an age of refinement. This barbarism in turn is dispersed, and then reappears; it is a continuous alternation of day and night.' At other times he gave expression to ideas of historical progress of the most categorical kind.

Voltaire was frequently inconsistent. This was not because his mind was 'a chaos of clear ideas', as some have suggested. It was because his mind was too vigorous to enjoy, or seek, the deadly repose of a system. He was too alive to the quiddities of human circumstances and too alert to the sufferings of individual human beings to subscribe unambiguously to any grand scheme of human progress. In this, he showed himself humbler than many amongst his contemporaries and his posterity. It is because he did not consistently share the wilful hopes of most Enlightenment thinkers in his day and ours that Voltaire's is a voice we can still hear.

The dark view of history and the human prospect to which – despite himself – Voltaire was inclined is not an incidental detail in his way of thinking. It flows from the

Enlightenment itself. In so far as Enlightenment thought is clear-eyed it must accept that civilization – as Enlightenment thinkers themselves understand it – is a rare and fragile artifice. The view of history adopted by Gibbon, Hume, Voltaire and other Enlightenment historians does not support the belief that civilization is the natural condition of human beings. After all, as these historians often remind us, slavery, tyranny and ignorance have been the lot of practically all human beings who have ever lived. Indeed, confronted with the record of the species, an impartial observer might reasonably conclude that barbarism is its natural state.

When it is followed intrepidly, the final result of Enlightenment thinking is not to keep alight the moral hopes bequeathed to the world by Christianity. As was understood by Nietzsche, who admired the Enlightenment and Voltaire for this very reason, it is to extinguish them. Yet, because it emerged from within Christendom, the Enlightenment could not help appealing to many of the hopes evoked by the faith it aimed to replace. It has always harboured expectations of progress for which there can be no place in a thoroughly naturalistic, truly post-Christian account of humankind and its place in the world.

Voltaire shared the hope of universal emancipation that Christianity had introduced into European life. Like other Enlightenment thinkers, he ascribed to the growth of knowledge the liberating role in human life that Christianity attributed to faith. But unlike many Enlightenment thinkers of his day and later, he did not value knowledge for its own sake. He viewed it instrumentally, as a means to greater human happiness. In his consistent emphasis on well-being as the criterion of value, Voltaire showed the deep influence on him of Epicurean thought. Like Epicurus, he was inclined to understand human happiness negatively, as the absence of suffering. Like Epicurus, he thought freedom from illusion and religious superstition was a vital precondition of this negative happiness. For him emancipation from false beliefs was not different from happiness but an ingredient in it.

Voltaire did not allow the secularized version of Christian providence to which he subscribed, along with other Enlightenment thinkers, to dull his sense of the random suffering of human life. There is a sharp contrast between Voltaire's constant stress on the primacy of well-being and Enlightenment thinkers such as Kant and Hegel for whom the development of human consciousness is the overriding good. Unlike these more programmatic Enlightenment thinkers, Voltaire could not bring himself to think of suffering as a means to any higher good.

In Voltaire we find an uncommonly candid mind coming up against contradictions in the Enlightenment that are no less insurmountable than those he mocked without mercy in Christianity. If, for Christians, the perfect goodness of God renders evil a mystery, for true believers in Enlightenment the goodness of human nature renders the evils of history inexplicable. From Voltaire to the present day, Enlightenment thinking is an attempt to construct a secular theodicy in which the evils of history are explained. The chief interest of Voltaire today may come from his struggle to reconcile this Enlightenment theodicy with the evident facts of human life.

The darker implications of Enlightenment thinking were evident to some of its greatest twentieth-century exponents. Sigmund Freud and Bertrand Russell never doubted that reason and civilization go against the grain. They scorned the utopias of Marx and Spencer; they rejected doctrines of human perfectibility. Neither of them found grounds to believe that the future of the species would be fundamentally different from its past. Freud confessed that consolation was something he could not offer mankind. Russell doubted that reason would ever be strong enough to withstand the force of destructive emotion. Resignation seems to have been their final mood. In this they followed Voltaire.

VOLTAIRE'S RELIGION

There were once many atheists among the Christians; they are now much fewer. It at first appears to be a paradox, but examination proves it to be a truth, that theology often threw men's minds into atheism, until philosophy at length drew them out of it.

Voltaire[6]

Voltaire said of the Church Fathers that they believed that the whole world ought to be as they were, and were therefore necessarily the enemies of the whole world until it was converted. The same was true of Voltaire himself, and remains true of his Enlightenment posterity today.

Voltaire's Enlightenment ideals led him to treat nearly all societies of which he had knowledge as approximations to – or, more often, departures from – civilization. He was a consistent advocate of religious toleration and a notable critic of Europocentrism. He found much that was valuable in many other cultures, ancient and modern. But ultimately he valued them not as ends in themselves, but as stepping-stones to a universal civilization. In consequence, he viewed ways of life incompatible with the Enlightenment not with toleration – as expressions of the variety of life of which a highly inventive animal is capable – but enmity. Like the Christians they reviled, Voltaire and other thinkers of the European Enlightenment have never accepted a diversity of cultures and values as an unalterable fact of human life. Still less have they welcomed it as desirable.

To be sure, the Enlightenment has never been a single, homogeneous movement. The Enlightenment took many different forms, depending on the circumstances and cultural contexts in which it arose. In its eighteenth-century manifestations it had many sources – John Locke's empiricist view of knowledge, the rationalism of Descartes, Pierre Bayle's scepticism, Newtonian science, Montesquieu's and Voltaire's fascination with non-European cultures, particularly Persia and China, and the continuing influence on these and other Enlightenment thinkers of theories of natural law – that were not always compatible. Enlightenment thinkers could be more or less optimistic about the future of the species. Many earlier Enlightenment or proto-Enlightenment thinkers – Spinoza and Montesquieu, for example – were comparatively free of the hubris of later thinkers such as Tom Paine and Auguste Comte. Again, theories of progress of the kinds advanced by Turgot and Condorcet were rejected by much of the Scottish Enlightenment. And, perhaps most importantly, the Enlightenment comprehended divergent attitudes to religion and morality. The atheism of d'Holbach and the rationalism of Descartes were anathema to Voltaire, and Kant repudiated Hume's moral scepticism in favour of an ideal of rational moral autonomy that Hume would have found incredible. In all these respects, and more, the Enlightenment was a far-flung and often highly quarrelsome family of thinkers and movements.

Yet there is no justification for the view – currently something of an orthodoxy amongst those who wish to support the Enlightenment without owning up to what it is that they are defending – that these thinkers had no goals or values in common. Nor is it true that they shared no common enterprise. On the contrary, whatever their many and sometimes large differences, all Enlightenment thinkers – from the French *philosophes*, the compilers of dictionaries and encyclopedias with whom the Enlightenment is most commonly identified, through Hume and Kant, to the nineteenth-century positivists, Marxists and liberals whose posterity we all are today – subscribed to a single project.

Enlightenment thinkers have always aimed to supplant the diverse traditions and religious beliefs by which humanity has hitherto been ruled with a new morality whose authority is rational and universal. Whether they grounded this morality in the requirements of reason, like Kant, or based it on the constancy of human nature, with Hume, the thinkers of the Enlightenment were at one in their conviction that the basic values of civilized human beings are essentially identical. This morality defines the values of the universal civilization for which all Enlightenment thinkers work. Without such a universal morality the Enlightenment project of a universal civilization is indefensible.

It is this faith in a universal civilization that the intellectual movement sometimes called the Counter-Enlightenment was concerned to attack. Like those of the Enlightenment, the thinkers of the Counter-Enlightenment were immensely diverse in their beliefs and circumstances; but in different ways they all sought to undermine the Enlightenment faith that civilized human beings are everywhere at bottom the same. In so doing they showed that they had penetrated to the common substratum that underlies all Enlightenment ideas, however diverse their surface appearances.

Vico's contention that historical epochs may be so different that their values cannot be recaptured without a tremendous effort of imagination, Herder's claim that different cultures may honour goods that cannot be combined and which are sometimes incommensurable, Pascal's distinction between *l'esprit de géométrie* and *l'esprit de finesse* and its corollary that truth cannot be contained within the confines of any system or discovered by applying any one method – such ideas are alien to the humanist spirit of the Enlightenment. They limit too narrowly what can be known by human beings and what can reasonably be hoped for them to be acceptable to any Enlightenment thinker.

In the eighteenth century, as today, those who hold to Enlightenment ideas cannot surrender the faith that human values vary only at the margins. They must cling to the belief that, at bottom, human ends are everywhere the same, diverging as much as they do only because of differences between cultures and gaps in human knowledge that can be overcome. But if history is an exfoliation of many cultures, rationally incomparable with one another in some centrally important respects, if the values of different epochs and peoples cannot always be ranked on a single scale but may be finally divergent and incompatible, if human knowledge itself cannot be unified but will remain always riddled with discontinuities and lacunae, then a universal civilization, founded on reason, is an impossibility. At any rate, if thinkers such as Pascal, Hamann, Vico and Herder are not entirely mistaken, a civilization of the sort that the *philosophes* projected cannot be realized without an unprecedented expansion of human knowledge and a desolating diminution in cultural diversity. Yet the ideal of such a universal civilization remains the Enlightenment project to this day.

When a reaction arose against Voltaire's ideas among Counter-Enlightenment thinkers such as J.G. Herder (who dismissed Voltaire – in terms that William Blake would not have found strange – as a 'senile child'), it was Voltaire's assumption that civilization was one and the same for all human beings, whatever their histories and cultures, that was the chief target of attack. Herder questioned the certainty, which Voltaire took from Christianity and from the central traditions of Greek philosophy, that there is a good life proper to all human beings, however seemingly diverse their cultures or natures. In late modern times, from the late nineteenth century to the present, that questioning has found issue in fascist and nationalist regimes and in postmodernist, fundamentalist and multiculturalist movements, which in their different and indeed conflicting ways are all children of the reaction against the Enlightenment.

For Voltaire civilization might be rare, and difficult to maintain for long; but its peaks are recognizably the same wherever they are climbed. When we read in Voltaire that there were only four great ages in which civilization flourished – the age of Alexander, the age of Augustus, Florence during the Renaissance and the age of Louis XIV in France – we smile; but some such view of history is still a conventional wisdom today. It underpins political projects as seemingly divergent as those of Jürgen Habermas and Francis Fukuyama, Friedrich Hayek and John Rawls.

Like Augustine and like Pascal, Voltaire accepted that humanity could not attain the good that it so clearly discerns. Yet with these great Christian thinkers, he was certain that the good was one, not many, and could not harbour irreconcilable conflicts. Along with Condorcet,

Diderot, Paine, Jefferson and many lesser projectors of what has been called 'the heavenly city of the eighteenth century philosophers',[7] Voltaire may sometimes have come close to despair at human stupidity. But he could never bring himself to doubt that a universal human civilization could be imagined and, in principle, constructed – if not now or soon then in some far-off future, if not completely and for ever then at least in part and for a while. In his unshakeable conviction that the good is one, universal and harmonious, Voltaire belongs with the past, with medieval and classical thinkers, such as Aquinas, Plato and the Stoics, not with the future in which we now live.

Voltaire's was neither a speculative nor a subversive mind. He lacked the intuitive insight into the deeper maladies of European life that made Rousseau an influence on all subsequent reflection. Voltaire was not uncritical of the civilization of his time. Like Freud after him, he thought the price it exacted in human suffering was high and could be reduced. But he never interrogated his ideal of civilization itself. He took for granted that the form of life of societies devoted to the growth of scientific knowledge and increasing power over nature was self-evidently superior to all others. In this certainty Voltaire only exemplifies an unquestioned dogma held in common by all the *philosophes*.

Of course, Voltaire was the first to admit that Enlightenment ideals must be adapted to circumstances. He recognized that the path of progress was far from being a straight line. Different modes of government were best in different times and places, various social institutions and religions necessary and useful in different societies. But the goal was the same for all humankind. Voltaire was a political relativist. He favoured enlightened despotism in some contexts, approximations to political liberty in others. But he was never an ethical pluralist. Without giving the matter much thought, Voltaire believed that the ends of reasonable people are everywhere roughly the same, and that they are reasonably harmonious with one another. Just as much as the Christians, he was certain that the human good was not many – as an unprejudiced view of history might suggest – but one.

As it does notoriously in Christianity, this conviction of Voltaire's came up against some familiar and awkward facts. For Voltaire, as for nearly all the *philosophes*, Nature – including human nature – was virtuous or at least innocent of evil, which came into the world only with error. But how to account for the amazing fertility and stubborn persistence of error? If, as the *philosophes* asserted in opposition to Christianity, human nature is not marked by original sin, why is it that human history is – as Voltaire vehemently insisted – a catalogue of errors, crimes and barbarous enthusiasms?

Enlightenment theories of progress are (among other things) an attempt to answer this question. Most represent history as a succession of developmental phases, driven on by the growth of knowledge. The idea of progress in history is not an inevitable part of Enlightenment thought. It is doubtful that it can be found in David Hume, the greatest philosopher of the Scottish Enlightenment and the eighteenth-century thinker who achieved the most complete transcendence of Christianity. Hume did not suppose that the species would in future achieve any degree of civilization higher than that which it had attained in the past. He believed that human history would be in future what it had been hitherto – a cycle of civilization and barbarism. We cannot hope to surpass the ancients, only – if we are wise and lucky – to match them. But like Voltaire, Hume was in

21

no doubt that civilization embodied the same values wherever and whenever it was to be found.

This article of faith – for it is hardly a truth that stares at us from history's blank face – is indispensable to the Enlightenment. Without it a universal civilization is mere cultural imperialism, no more admirable or rationally defensible than the meddling schemes of Christian missionaries.

The universal civilization for which the *philosophes* worked is a civilization of a definite type. Its foundations are the growth of knowledge and the domination of nature. It is hostile not only to cultures in which a transcendental faith is central, but also those that seek harmony with the earth. As its most candid partisans have always admitted or boasted, such an ideal of civilization can be achieved only at the cost of uprooting nearly all the cultural traditions that human beings have contrived for themselves.

Among nineteenth- and twentieth-century thinkers, it is an ideal commonly buttressed by a faith in progress. But it is faith in universal emancipation rather than in progress that links the Enlightenment with Christianity. Whether or not Enlightenment thinkers subscribe to any conception of progress, they are ruled by a vision of the emancipation of humankind through the growth of knowledge.

The faith of the *philosophes* that humankind can be led to a condition of universal freedom separates them from the ancients whom they admired and joins them with the Christians whom they despised. Voltaire had nothing but contempt for the Christian project of theodicy. He was especially scornful of Leibniz's justification of the misfortunes of human life as necessary evils. Leibniz had argued in his *Essais de Théodicée* (1710) that the evils of the world are necessary features of it, since there is nothing without a reason. Leibniz appears to be suggesting that this must be 'the best of all possible worlds' because it is, in fact, the only possible world. A similar view had been expressed by Alexander Pope in his *Essay on Man*, when he wrote that 'One truth is clear, "Whatever is, is right".'

Pope's optimism had had some appeal to Voltaire when he read his poems with Mme du Châtelet at Cirey. But Voltaire's deistic confidence in a providential design was not impervious to experience. It was shaken to its foundations by the Lisbon earthquake of 1 November (All Saints' Day) 1755, in which over 20,000 people perished. The shock of the Lisbon earthquake moved Voltaire to publish in 1756 a heartfelt long *Poème sur le désastre de Lisbonne*, and in 1757 to begin writing his most famous and best literary work, an ingenious and moving *conte philosophique*, *Candide*, published in 1759 to Europe-wide acclaim.

In *Candide* Voltaire mocked Leibniz's attempted demonstration that the evils of the world were necessary to its perfection, satirizing his 'principle of sufficient reason' as a rationalistic reformulation of Christian providence. Through the comic character of the obtuse optimist, Dr Pangloss, Voltaire added a new epithet of abuse, 'panglossian', to European vocabularies. Part of the interest of Voltaire to us today comes from his struggle, reflected in *Candide* and others of his philosophical tales, to reconcile his Deist-Enlightenment faith with the random misery of human life.

When Candide meets a raddled, syphilitic beggar, 'all covered with sores, his eyes glazed, the end of his nose eaten away, his mouth askew, his teeth black, racked by a violent cough and spitting out teeth with every spasm', he is horrified to discover that it is his old tutor, Dr Pangloss. On hearing Pangloss's account of how he got the pox – from Paquette, 'who was made a present of it by a very knowledgeable Franciscan who got it from a captain in the cavalry, who owed it to a marchioness, who had it from a page, who had caught it from a Jesuit, who, during his noviciate, had inherited it in a direct line from one of Christopher Columbus's shipmates' – Candide cries: 'O Pangloss! What a strange genealogy! Was it not the devil who began it?' But the metaphysician is unperturbed:

'Not at all,' replied the great man. 'It was an indispensable part of the best of all worlds, a necessary ingredient. For if Columbus, on an island in the Americas, had not caught this disease which poisons the spring of procreation, which often even prevents procreation, and which is evidently the opposite of what nature intended, we would have neither chocolate nor cochineal. Moreover, one must remember that up to now this disease has been unique to the inhabitants of our continent, like controversy. The Turks, the Indians, the Persians, the Chinese, the Siamese, the Japanese, they have all yet to know it. But there is sufficient reason for them to know it in their turn a few centuries hence. In the meantime it is making spectacular progress among our population, and especially among those great armies of fine, upstanding, well-bred mercenaries who decide the destiny of nations.'[8]

Whether the examples he chose were the introduction of syphilis into Europe or the Lisbon earthquake, Voltaire aimed to render ridiculous and disgusting the consolations for suffering provided by Christianity and metaphysicians such as Leibniz. As Voltaire makes Candide exclaim: 'If this is the best of all possible worlds, then what must the others be like?'

Yet his scorn for Christian doctrines of providence never led Voltaire to abandon the Enlightenment theodicy of universal emancipation. In Voltaire, to be sure, this was not the historical theodicy of Kant, Hegel, Marx or John Stuart Mill, in which human life is redeemed by the achievement of ever higher stages of human consciousness. Voltaire was too earthy in his sense of life to be tempted by the idea that any such achievement could redeem life's miseries. Like Epicurus, he prized knowledge as a means to happiness, not as a compensation for misery. He never supposed that human life could be unalloyed pleasure. As he writes in the *Philosophical Dictionary*, in the section on 'Good':

> If the name of happiness is meant to be applied to some pleasures which are diffused over human life, there is in fact, we must admit, happiness. If the name attaches only to one pleasure always permanent, or to a continued though varied range of delicious experiences, then happiness belongs not to this terraqueous globe. Go and seek for it elsewhere.[9]

There is nothing utopian in Voltaire's conception of human well-being. He is a follower of Epicurus in his sober and moderate understanding of human happiness. Voltaire is an unequivocal meliorist. Yet his commitment to the alleviation of the human lot is not one that Epicurus or any other pre-Christian thinker could have recognized or shared. It is a species of hedonism shot through with Christian ambitions for humanity.

The ancient hedonists had no hopes for the species, only for a lucky few of its members. They took for granted that the majority of humankind were too unfortunate – too hard-pressed, too poor or too unintelligent – to be other than wretched. Their meliorism was confined to individual lives, and to those of a few, whom fortune had blessed. To write off the mass of the species in this way is difficult for anyone reared in a Christian tradition, and it was intolerable for Voltaire. Voltaire's meliorism was always a project of improvement for humankind, never merely for the few. He ended *Candide* by putting into its hero's mouth the words 'We must tend our gardens.' But he would have been horrified if, as it did for the Epicureans, this were to mean enjoying the company of friends who have retreated from the world, and turning one's back on the sufferings of the rest.

In this, despite himself, Voltaire followed the Christians, not the Epicureans. For it is in their faith in the salvation of all humankind that both Christianity and the Enlightenment differ from more ancient philosophies and religions. Without that dubious faith Voltaire's hopes of a universal civilization are vain. Like much else in the Enlightenment, they are the hopes of Christianity, emptied of transcendence and attached improbably to the human species.

Voltaire aspired to be a pagan, but the hope of universal emancipation was not one shared by any pagan thinker. It comes not from Plato or Aristotle, Epicurus or the Stoics, but from the Christian faith that all human beings can be saved. Voltaire's view of the intellectual powers of most people was never high, but like the Christian apologists whom he loved to deride, he did not doubt that a single way of life was best for all humankind. At the end of the twentieth century, this faith of Voltaire's is difficult to share. Indeed, for some of us, it is not easy to comprehend.

Perhaps it was inevitable that, in seeking to replace Christianity, Voltaire's Enlightenment creed should come to resemble it. At any rate it was essential for him to discredit Christianity. He believed a modern civilization was incompatible with the power of the Church and with the appeal to mystery on which Christianity is based. For Voltaire, a modern society must of necessity be secular.

Traditional faiths are bound to die away and – Voltaire was convinced – be replaced by a scientific worldview.

For Voltaire, as for all the *philosophes* and their followers today, it was an axiom of the modern outlook that the authority of the Church must yield to that of science. Yet Voltaire never imagined that modern societies would be lacking in religious feeling. Indeed, sometimes almost eclipsed by the intensity of his enmity to Christianity, a major part of his life's work was inventing a religion for moderns.

With Benjamin Franklin, Voltaire subscribed to one of the Enlightenment's most fantastic projects – a rational religion. Voltaire was a Deist. He believed that the existence of a Supreme Being can be inferred by natural reason from the evidences of design in the world. In the entry on 'Sects' in the *Philosophical Dictionary*, Voltaire asks rhetorically:

> What would be the true religion, if Christianity did not exist? That in which there would be no sects; that in which all minds necessarily agreed. Now, in what doctrine are all minds agreed? In the adoration of one God, and in probity. All the philosophers who have professed a religion have said at all times – There is a God, and he must be just. Behold then the universal religion, established throughout all times and among all men!

Unlike more venturesome spirits among the *philosophes*, such as La Mettrie, d'Holbach and de Sade, Voltaire rejected explanations of belief in a Supreme Being which derived it from ignorance, the feebleness of the average human mind or the self-interest of priests and kings. He considered the worship of a Supreme Being to be both natural and reasonable. His single-minded opposition to Christianity was not an expression of hostility to religion, for Voltaire was a man of unselfconscious, if shallow, religious feeling. Voltaire devoted so much of his life to attacking Christianity because he believed Christianity to be the greatest obstacle in the way of the civilization to which he aspired.

Where did Voltaire acquire his hostility to Christianity? It is sometimes suggested that Voltaire's taste for freethinking came by way of his admiration for the English Deists. It is true that, a life-long and self-avowed Anglomaniac, Voltaire was influenced by the English Deists' demand for freedom of thought and expression in all matters of religious belief. He admired their commitment to reasonableness in religion and revered them as advocates of toleration. But Voltaire's thinking about religion was a development of a long-standing French tradition. The writings of the English Deists strengthened, but they did not originate, Voltaire's disposition to freethinking.

Voltaire's attitudes to Christianity had a more important French source in 'the Temple' – a sodality of freethinkers and libertines, based in a thirteenth-century castle in Paris and led by Philippe de Vendôme, Grand Prior of the Knights of Malta, to which Voltaire was introduced as a young man. The society of 'the Temple' kept alive the tradition of the seventeenth-century French *libertins érudits*, a loose grouping that embraced figures such as Molière and Cyrano de Bergerac. The *libertins érudits* were themselves inspired by the sixteenth-century *nouveaux pyrrhoniens*, so called because they sought to revive the radically sceptical philosophy of Pyrrho of Elis and his followers in the ancient Greek school of Sextus Empiricus.

Among the *nouveaux pyrrhoniens*, the great essayist Michel de Montaigne and his disciple Pierre Charron, author of the immensely influential manual of the new Pyrrhonism, *La Sagesse*, were a profound influence on the *libertins érudits*, as were Bayle, Gassendi and Mersenne. At the same time, the hedonist and materialist doctrines of Epicurus and Lucretius were equally or more important in shaping the views of the freethinkers of the Temple.

Pyrrhonian scepticism was not necessarily hostile to faith. Indeed, by humiliating reason and deflating the pretensions of human knowledge, Montaigne and Charron contrived to reaffirm the mysteries of Christianity. New Pyrrhonian writers such as François La Mothe le Vayer produced a species of sceptical and fideistic Christian apologetics reminiscent of Pascal. In an irony of intellectual history, David Hume's revival of Pyrrhonist arguments for the frailty of human reason was used by fideist thinkers such as J.G. Hamann as a support for religious faith. Through these Counter-Enlightenment thinkers Hume's Pyrrhonism was one of the sources of Kierkegaard's elevation of faith over reason.

The Pyrrhonian tradition in French free thought was not a strong strand in the society of the Temple. It found few echoes in Voltaire. His view of scientific knowledge and moral judgement was not sceptical but empirical and commonsensical. In this and other respects Voltaire's outlook was Epicurean, not Pyrrhonian. He valued knowledge instrumentally, for its contribution to human well-being, not for its own sake. He took human knowledge to be limited and surrounded by ignorance. But its sources in the senses, in common experience and in the methods of the sciences, he viewed as unproblematic. Voltaire was not driven to scepticism, as Pyrrhonians commonly have been, by a vain search for truth. Like Epicurus, he was confident that we know enough to be happy – if only we rid ourselves of superstition. In the notably strikingly unsceptical doctrine of Deism, Voltaire thought he had found a religion without superstition.

His defence of Deism is notably feeble. He had been

much impressed by Newton's *Principia Mathematica* (1687), in which the clock-like workings of the universe are invoked to support the existence of a divine Clock-Maker. Voltaire invokes variations on this argument from design, which uses order in the world as evidence for an Orderer, without answering cogent objections to that venerable reasoning. He could not have replied to Hume's devastating critique of the argument from design in his *Dialogues on Natural Religion*, since it was published posthumously in 1779, after Voltaire had died; but he could have attempted a coherent response to the powerful criticism of arguments from design presented by d'Holbach in his *Système de la nature*. In fact, though he tried to parry some of d'Holbach's blows, Voltaire attached little weight to any of these arguments. As he did when he invoked common judgement to give a content to morality, he made no attempt to show that belief in a Supreme Being is reasonable, but appealed instead to a consensus in support of that belief amongst reasonable people.

He also argued that Deism was humanity's first faith. Influenced by Bolingbroke and Pope, Voltaire contended that belief in a single Supreme Being was the original faith of the earliest humans, and was relinquished only with the growth of priestly castes. It is hard to understand how he squared this claim with what he knew of Greek and Roman polytheism. Nor is it easily reconciled with his admiration for Hume, who had argued persuasively in his *Natural History of Religion* that polytheism, not monotheism, is the aboriginal religion of mankind.

It is impossible to square Voltaire's bizarre claim that the religion of savage humanity was monotheistic with his conviction that the intellectual powers of human beings grow stronger in proportion as they become more civilized. How does Voltaire account for the historical fact, which was as evident to him as it is to us, that among the Romans and the Greeks polytheism and civilization went hand in hand? How could the perception of a Supreme Being grow fainter as civilization and the human mind advanced?

In fact Voltaire knew little of the beliefs of archaic humanity, and cared less. In his view 'primitive' peoples belonged to the infancy of the species. Their view of the world was a compound of fear, confusion and crude analogical reasonings, worth studying by civilized people, if at all, only as a reminder of how far intellectual progress had since advanced. Remarkably, Voltaire seems not to have noticed how this standard Enlightenment view of traditional peoples – devastatingly criticized by Wittgenstein in his *Remarks on Frazer's Golden Bough*[10] – clashed with his account of their religious beliefs.

Voltaire's inability to give a credible account of the place of monotheism in the natural history of religion does more than weaken his defence of Deism. It illuminates a contradiction in his view of human nature. Pascal posed the problem in which Voltaire's thought floundered with his usual unsurpassable clarity: 'Habit is a second nature that destroys the first. But what is nature? Why is habit not natural? I am very much afraid that nature itself is only a first habit, just as habit is a second nature.'[11]

The difficulties of Voltaire's religion come at two levels. The first have to do with the infirmities of the mass of humankind, and were well understood by Voltaire himself. The second concern the foundations of his project of a universal morality, and are fatal to his and any other Enlightenment project.

Voltaire held that human beings cleave naturally to a reasonable worship of a Supreme Being; but, as he himself constantly reminds us, their history shows them exchanging one fanatical religion for another. If the human species is by nature rational, what accounts for its history? Does that history not show Voltaire's conception of human nature to be itself unreasonable?

Volaire often doubted that humankind at large could be trusted with the truth of Deism. Like many of the *philosophes*, he was tempted by the idea of the noble lie, of a religion or mythology manufactured to keep the majority in check. He always retained an acute sense of the civil functions of religion and deplored atheism not only because he judged it false, but on account of the risks he believed it posed to social peace.

In his later years Voltaire concluded that the cause of progress might be best served by educating the people in the truth – the truth of Deism. Yet, admirably candid, Voltaire's assessment of the majority of the species was never flattering. As he wrote to d'Alembert: 'As for the *canaille*, I have no concern with it; it will always remain *canaille*.'[12] In the margin of an English book, Voltaire wrote: 'Natural religion for the magistrates, damned stuff for the mob'. He set out his views more extensively in his *Notebooks*: 'It is a matter of indifference to the unthinking masses whether we give them truths or errors to believe, wisdom or madness; they will follow one or the other equally; they are only blind machines.'[13] There is a celebrated anecdote that, when d'Alembert and Condorcet made conversational sallies against religion while dining at Ferney, Voltaire cautioned them, sent the servants out of the room, and declared, 'Now, gentlemen, you may continue. I was only afraid of having my throat cut tonight.'

A low opinion of the human majority is not uncommon amongst Enlightenment thinkers. In our time it was echoed by Russell and Freud. Both tried to account for the irrationality of the mass of mankind by a theory of unconscious mental life. They speculated that repressed emotions and memories worked beneath the surface of conscious thought to deform and distort the understanding. Both advocated what Freud called a dictatorship of reason – the conscious control of the instincts and emotions. In this Freud and Russell were typical thinkers of the Enlightenment, distinguished from their more conventional *confrères* only by the frankness of their pessimism.

The natural implication of a low view of one's fellows is a theory of education or, for those less sanguine regarding the educability of the majority of the species, a theory of government by élites. Both are to be found in Voltaire. He would not have dissented from Maynard Keynes's mature view that 'civilisation was a thin and precarious crust erected by the personality and the will of a very few, and only maintained by rules and conventions skilfully put across and guilefully preserved'.[14]

It is not the intellectual and moral frailties of ordinary human nature that pose the most serious threat to Voltaire's Enlightenment ideals. It is irreconcilable conflicts among human values. Why should we follow Voltaire in valuing the growth of scientific knowledge over a stable society? A cosmopolitan civilization over local ways of life? Voltaire has no account of ethics that might confer the imprimatur of reason on his ideals. Lacking any unique or universal authority, they can claim only to embody one way of life that human beings may find worth living.

Like that of his principal mentor in philosophy, Locke, Voltaire's account of moral judgement is undermined by his empiricist account of knowledge. For Voltaire, as for Locke, all knowledge is grounded in observation. But if we rely on observation alone, we find (as Montaigne noted) not so much a consensus on the content of natural law as a miscellany of conflicting moral beliefs and practices. How can an empiricist, committed to observation as the sole source of reliable knowledge, make of that chaos a coherent unity?

Locke solved the problem by deriving morality from a divine will that was revealed in the Bible. That recourse is not open to Voltaire. He can do no more than appeal to the common view of men of good judgement – *le bon sens*. But that is to pass over the problem, not to resolve it.

In truth Voltaire could not have solved it. His appeal to common judgement is circular. What counts as a reasonable man? And what is to be done when reasonable men disagree? Voltaire's appeal to a common human consensus in support of his ethical beliefs is peculiarly unconvincing. His usual view of human beliefs is that overall they are a tissue of absurdities. How are we to know which universal human beliefs are true, and which merely universal superstitions?

Belief in what Voltaire judges are absurdities is not confined to the ignorant masses. The majority of reflective people who have ever lived have subscribed to one or other of the faiths that Voltaire considered absurd. Equally, many cultivated people in the past have held to moral beliefs that Voltaire could not but find monstrous. The Stoics, who appealed to a universal consensus to support their moral beliefs, saw nothing wrong in slavery. Nor did the early Christians. The truth is that consensus alone is too unstable a thing in which to ground any but the barest minimum of human values. In any case, an appeal to the universal agreement of humankind does not fit well with Voltaire's contempt for most of what has hitherto passed for human knowledge. Nor can it be squared with the understanding of the values of other cultures that the Enlightenment itself has given us.

Of course, this is not to say that there are no universal human values. Manifestly there are generically human evils. Hunger, pain and violent death are misfortunes for all human beings whatever their cultural differences. Equally there are universal human goods – food, peace, sexual and familial love and friendship, among others. But these universal values are found in many moralities. They do not dictate a single way of life as the best for all humanity. Still less do they show the Enlightenment ideal of civilization to be that one way of life.

Voltaire wrote that just as there is only one geometry so there is only one morality. But an irreducible plurality of moralities – or, for that matter, of geometries – defeats this certainty. For it is not only that equally reflective and well-informed people make different moral judgements. Often they understand the human good itself differently.

Deep value-conflict of this kind defeated a greater Enlightenment thinker than Voltaire. David Hume perceived more clearly than any Enlightenment thinker that an empiricist view of knowledge entails ethical scepticism. He was able nevertheless to affirm that civilized values are everywhere the same because he exaggerated the constancy of human nature. Curiously, for he was a great historian as well as an incomparably great philosopher, Hume underestimated the differences among cultures. Perhaps it was no accident that he did, for if he had not done so, he could not have held to his faith that civilization everywhere embodied the same values.

For Voltaire morality had not yet become questionable. He was confident that there were true ethical beliefs and he had no doubt that he knew what they were. He did not inquire how large a portion of his moral certitude was owed to Christian ethics. It did not occur to him that European morality would be much altered by the passing of Christianity.

Nor did Voltaire ask what would become of the universal

claims of European civilization once it had become definitively post-Christian. Like Rousseau, whom he loathed, Voltaire thought that only prejudice and self-interest prevented human beings from reaching agreement about the good. And, like Rousseau, he thought the human good was the same for all.

In his conviction that truth in ethics is self-evident to persons of unclouded judgement, Voltaire looks backward to medieval and early modern ideas of natural law, not forward to the late modern condition of ethical and cultural pluralism. He never doubted the authority of morality. In this curious lack of ethical scepticism, Voltaire's Age of Enlightenment is further from us than early modernity, which begins – in Machiavelli, Montaigne and Hobbes – with a questioning of morality.

VOLTAIRE'S POLITICS

What is toleration? It is the appurtenance of humanity. We are all full of weakness and errors; let us mutually pardon each other our follies, – it is the first law of nature.

Voltaire[15]

Like all the *philosophes*, Voltaire worked for the emancipation of the species; but he did not suppose that this meant the universal establishment of a single political regime. Throughout his active life he was committed to the same liberal political values; but he never imagined that these political ideals could, or should, be embodied in one mode of government. At times he opted for enlightened despotism, flirting with Catherine the Great and Frederick of Prussia, at others he supported constitutional monarchy.

Here and there in Voltaire's writings we can even find some favourable references to democracy. (Yet he never shared civic republican beliefs about the inherent virtue of popular self-government.)

Voltaire's views on what was the best regime changed greatly over his long, busy and varied life. But his life-long political flexibility was not a symptom of inveterate opportunism. It is true that Voltaire enjoyed the company of men and women of power and sought their favour. He was not too scrupulous to flatter those whom he courted. But he did not conceal his views to avoid displeasing them. Voltaire's support for diverse regimes in different times and places does not show him trimming his opinions to suit his patrons. It was an application of an unchanging outlook. Voltaire was not an opportunist but a political relativist.

The enduring interest of Voltaire's political thought derives from its fusion of political relativism with liberal morality. Voltaire's liberalism shows how a pragmatic and instrumental approach to regimes and institutions can be combined with principled commitment to liberal values. It is not only that Voltaire understood that liberal values justified different strategies in varying circumstances. He saw that the histories and environments of different peoples could warrant different regimes indefinitely.

Voltaire admired English institutions inordinately; but he did not think of transposing them to France. He believed that the traditions, the mores, the climates, of different countries made diverse modes of government desirable in them. In this belief, Voltaire was at one with Montesquieu, with whom he differed on many other, less fundamental matters.

Voltaire's thought does not contain a systematic political theory of the kind we find in Hobbes or Rousseau. But that does not mean his thinking was unsystematic. Much of it is a criticism of grand political theories that neglect the importance of history and circumstance. Voltaire was particularly critical of doctrines that ground the legitimacy of political regimes in the requirements of a state of nature. As a political relativist, he was hostile to all such arguments. Indeed, in its more theoretical aspects, Voltaire's political thought is a sustained criticism of the uses of the state of nature in political thought, especially in that of his famous contemporary, J.-J. Rousseau.

Few writers have ever displayed more withering contempt for Rousseau than Voltaire. He thanked Rousseau for sending him his 'new book against the human race', the *Discourse on Inequality*, with the dismissive observation that it made him 'want to walk on all fours again'. There were many reasons for Voltaire's contempt for Rousseau, some of them personal, some accidental. In their temperaments Voltaire and Rousseau were close to being opposites. Voltaire's shrewd worldliness and unfailing practicality, his pragmatic concern with feasible improvements, his scorn for nobility of feeling divorced from effective action were marks of a disposition deeply at odds with Rousseau's.

The Imagist poet T.E. Hulme[16] distinguished between the 'classical' mind, which views humankind as a species from whose limited and constant nature something of worth can be extracted only by long discipline and intelligent organization, and the 'romantic' mind, which views humanity as a reservoir of infinite possibilities that society has somehow always thwarted. Nietzsche framed a similar contrast:

> The state of nature is terrible, man is a beast of prey. Our civilisation represents a tremendous triumph over this beast-of-prey nature; thus argued Voltaire ... Rousseau: the rule based on feeling; nature as the source of justice; man perfects himself to the extent to which he

approaches nature (according to Voltaire, the extent to which he moves away from nature). The very same epochs are for one ages of the progress of humanity; for the other, times when injustice and inequality grow worse ... Voltaire ... fights for ... the cause of taste, of science, of the arts, of progress itself and civilisation. The defense of providence by Rousseau (against the pessimism of Voltaire): he needed God in order to be able to cast a curse upon society and civilisation ... *Romanticism à la Rousseau.*[17]

In Hulme's and Nietzsche's terms, Voltaire embodied the classical spirit and Rousseau the romantic. To be sure, it is a distinction that fails to capture some ironies in the careers of the two thinkers. Rousseau, an enemy of modernity, expressed its spirit far better than did Voltaire, its self-conscious exemplar. He was rewarded for his diagnosis of the ills of civilization by an influence in the nineteenth and twentieth centuries that far exceeded Voltaire's. Moreover, Rousseau was far from being at all times an undisciplined romantic. His writings on particular countries, such as Poland, show evidence of sober and realistic thought. Nevertheless, the distinction between classical and romantic minds highlights some genuine and profound differences in the two thinkers' views of human nature and society.

Rousseau believed that human beings were corrupted by social institutions; Voltaire thought they were civilized by them. Rousseau castigated the institution of property as a primary cause of corruption, oppression and privation; for Voltaire, the institution of property was an emblem of civilization, a mark of individual freedom and a precondition of the creation of wealth. For Rousseau, 'natural man' stood for what was simple, authentic and sincere in human beings; Voltaire saw 'natural man' as merely lacking in refinement. Voltaire did not deny the existence of natural man. But he insisted that the point of civilization was to make something of him.

Underlying these differences are different accounts of natural man and the worth of civilization. Voltaire did not develop a single, coherent account of the relations of nature and civilization. At times he viewed nature through the lens of Epicurus, in which it was seen simply, as the universe in which we find ourselves. When he understood nature in these Epicurean terms, Voltaire was sharply critical of civilization as he found it. Actually existing civilizations had diminished the natural pleasures of human life and increased the pains by their adherence to the superstitions of Christianity. In this mood, Voltaire was not so far removed from Rousseau as he liked to believe.

In other moods Voltaire thought of the state of nature as impoverished and – above all – uncivilized. He was scornful of the view that the evils of society come from its departures from nature. As one of the interlocutors says in Voltaire's book of political and philosophical dialogues, *ABC*, undoubtedly speaking for Voltaire himself:

> Good houses, good clothing, a good standard of living, with good laws and freedom are better than want, anarchy and slavery. Those who are unhappy with London just have to go off to the Orkneys; there they will live as we used to in London in Caesar's time; they'll eat oat bread, cut each other's throats for sun-dried fish and a straw hut. Those who recommend it should set an example.[18]

Here Voltaire scoffs at Rousseau's neo-primitivist view, in which civilization is a corruption of the state of nature. Without going so far as to portray the state of nature as an evil, Voltaire insists that practically everything worthwhile in human life necessitates a departure from it. So far Voltaire agrees with Hobbes. But his view of the state of nature is not so dark. Hobbes saw it as a condition of rivalry and poverty – an incommodious war of all against all. In such a condition, Hobbes argued, it was rational for human beings to compete in ways that flouted the virtues and even harmed their self-interest. Here Hobbes had more than an inkling of the paradoxes of rational action captured in the Prisoner's Dilemma and other insights of the twentieth-century theory of games. There is none of this in Voltaire.

As Voltaire grew older he became increasingly inclined to determinism, perhaps because he believed it followed from the Newtonian, scientific view of the world. He seems not to have perceived any tension between his determinism regarding human beings and his political commitment to human emancipation. Yet the deterministic scientific account of nature to which he was increasingly disposed offered no support to Voltaire's humanitarian ideals. As de Sade discerned, an amoral, deterministic account of nature could as well sanction torture, slavery and murder as freedom, sympathy or human solidarity.[19] When nature is emptied of ethical norms, no way of life can claim nature's authority, for there is none that nature forbids. In that case, civilization is no better than barbarism. Voltaire's Enlightenment ideals are then just one way in which humans can live – if they wish.

Voltaire was clear that Enlightenment values do not demand the universal imposition of a single political regime. But he could not allow his relativism about political regimes to engulf the values that defined civilization itself. For him, every civilization was a token of a single type. History might echo with the tongues of many incommensurable cultures; but civilization spoke with one voice. For most practical purposes, Voltaire was confident that he was that voice. But he was unable to show why civilization as he understood it should have universal authority over the diversity of human cultures. He could not show why the diversity of cultures should not be regarded as pre-eminently *natural* for human beings.

Because what it signifies is essentially plural, the very idea of culture was alien to Voltaire's way of thinking. Contrary to the Enlightenment dichotomy of civilization and barbarism, the notion of culture implies that human beings have contrived in the past, and will in future invent, many different ways of living well. Voltaire's account of nature and civilization would have been more coherent if he had been willing to extend the scope of his relativism by acknowledging a plurality of cultures; but the mocking certainty with which he carried off his sallies against the *ancien régime* could scarcely have survived such an admission. In the end, Voltaire's idea of civilization was not a category in a philosophical argument. It was a rallying cry in a campaign.

The case of Jean Calas shows Voltaire in his role as a partisan in the battle for civilization. Calas was a Protestant Toulouse merchant whose son was baptized into the Roman Catholic church in order to practise as a lawyer. The son seems to have become depressed and committed suicide by hanging himself. Calas may have lost his life partly through his love for his son. He appears to have tried to conceal the cause of his death in order to spare him the customary treatment of suicides in Toulouse at that time, in which their bodies were stripped naked and dragged through the streets.

Calas was accused of his son's murder. He was subjected to judicial torture, found guilty and sentenced to be broken on the wheel and then strangled. The trial took place in an atmosphere of intense religious tension, which partly reflected Toulouse's history as the site of a massacre of Huguenots in 1562, and was conducted with slight regard to procedure and evidence. Nevertheless the sentence was carried out in March 1762. Voltaire took up the case and made it a scandal of European proportions. As a result of his involvement the verdict on Jean Calas was overturned in 1765 and Madame Calas received compensation from the King.

It was in battles such as the Calas case that Voltaire's ideal of civilization revealed its central meaning – toleration and the rule of law. Voltaire thought of institutions and regimes as instruments for the protection of these liberal values. For him enlightened despotism was preferable to lawless democracy, aristocratic privilege to republican virtue, if they served better these values of civilization. The best regime was always that which best promoted civilization. But what that regime was depended on time, place and circumstance.

Voltaire was a political relativist. At the same time he was a liberal. He sought to limit the arbitrariness of political power by subjecting it to law. Above all, he was concerned that the power of the state not be used in the service of comprehensive doctrines such as Christianity. Like generations of liberal thinkers after him, Voltaire's political ideals were liberty and toleration. He differed from twentieth-century liberals in his untroubled acceptance of natural inequalities and of the social inequalities that flow from them. Voltairian liberalism has no special tenderness to equality.

Voltaire was a perceptive critic of the mercantilist economic theories of his day, which equated the wealth of a state with its holdings of precious metals. He maintained that wealth consisted not in stores of gold or silver, but in a hard-working and skilful labour force and a high standard of living. In an immensely popular and lucrative pamphlet, *L'homme aux quarante écus*, whose success led to two booksellers being pilloried and sent to the galleys by the Paris parlement, Voltaire satirized the economic doctrines of the Physiocrats and attacked the inequities of the French system of taxation.

Voltaire ridiculed the economic orthodoxies of his day, scorning them as rationalizations for exploitation. Yet he was opposed to all schemes of economic levelling. Writing to d'Alembert in 1757, Voltaire even opposed the education of labourers, since its effect would be to 'spoil them for the plough'. (Later, however, he founded a free school at Ferney for the children of his workers.) Throughout his life he was hostile to proposals for egalitarian redistribution.

Voltaire's hostility to ideals of economic equality had many sources. Against Rousseau he held that security in the possession of private property was a prerequisite of civilization. In his argument against Rousseau, Voltaire appealed primarily to incentives rather than to a natural right to private property. He believed that, without security in the benefits that private property brings, the impulse to improve their circumstances dries up in most people. It is an argument that shows the importance Voltaire attached to economic considerations in human conduct. No doubt wisely, he never doubted that the motive of self-enrichment accounts for a great deal in political and religious life. He defended private property as a social institution that turns this egoistic passion to public benefit.

Against the *ancien régime* Voltaire believed that careers should be open to all talents. That meant that able individuals should be free to earn – and keep – large rewards. Voltaire's low view of the mass of humankind made him suspicious of any scheme of economic reform whose feasibility depended on altruism. In his entry on

'Equality' in the *Philosophical Dictionary* he declared that most human beings are born idle and the rest domineering. Given these facts of human nature, economic inequality – provided it was not extreme and there was a reasonable prospect of persons of talent becoming rich – was an engine of improvement. Here, as elsewhere, Voltairian liberalism is undogmatic and empirical. Like Mandeville, Voltaire was ready to defend the utility of luxury as a source of employment for the poor and a stimulus to the development of taste. He had no truck with a priori notions of economic equality. It is hard to imagine him having any time for John Rawls's Rousseauesque 'theory of justice'.

Voltaire's liberalism has some advantages over later liberalisms. For Enlightenment *lumières* in the late twentieth century, it appears self-evident that civilization goes with only one regime, liberal democracy. Some, such as Francis Fukuyama, have gone so far as to represent 'democratic capitalism' as 'the final form of human government'. By contrast, for Voltaire there was nothing self-evidently legitimate in democracy. He viewed it, as he did every other kind of regime, in instrumental terms. He judged democratic institutions by their contribution to human wellbeing. Theories of a natural right to popular government had no appeal to him. In this he is at one with a good many early Enlightenment thinkers and with most liberal political philosophers up to and including John Stuart Mill.

Unlike subsequent Enlightenment thinkers such as Marx and Hayek, Voltaire did not view history in a teleological perspective. If he hoped that all peoples would converge in a global civilization, he never imagined that this meant a single regime. Dogmatic in the extreme in his view of civilization, he was extremely pragmatic in his view of its political embodiments. Voltaire could not have fallen into Fukuyama's sorry confusion of liberal civilization with 'democratic capitalism'. For him it was self-evident that the turns of history are too complicated and the fortunes of regimes too particular and accidental for any such vulgar equation to be possible.

Voltaire criticized the inequities of the mercantilist economies of his day; but he was always clear that civilization could go with a variety of economic systems. Variations of climate and cultural history could make all the difference. He saw that the meritocratic statism he admired in China would be a recipe for corruption in France. No economic system was useful everywhere.

Voltaire's views on economic matters are often compared with those of Adam Smith. In regard to policy the comparison may not be entirely misleading. Both thinkers attacked many of the same restraints on enterprise. Both were advocates or economic freedom and critics of *dirigisme*. For all that, Voltaire was not a Smithian economic liberal. Adam Smith's invisible hand smacked too much of Christian providence to be congenial to Voltaire. It traded on a harmony of self-interest with virtue and the common good for which Voltaire, like Mandeville, found slight evidence in history or common experience.

In economic policy Voltaire's posterity is not to be found in the school of classical liberals that elevated *laissez-faire* to the status of a dogma. It is among the British Utilitarians, such as Jeremy Bentham and John Stuart Mill, who argued that the non-interference of government in economic life was only a rule of thumb. Though Voltaire had no theory of morality comparable with that of these Utilitarian thinkers, his view of political and economic systems was through and through instrumental. The test for all of them was whether they helped humanity to be (as he put it) 'a little less miserable'. (Like Bentham and J.S. Mill, Voltaire did not confine his concern to human misery. He was an early defender of the welfare of other animal species.)

Voltaire did not try to work out how this instrumental view was to be squared with his appeals to natural law. But it was a utilitarian concern with the reduction of suffering rather than his inheritances from the natural law tradition that underpinned Voltaire's moral judgements and his reformist campaigns.

Few liberal thinkers have ever been less doctrinaire than Voltaire. He never forgot that regimes and systems, political or economic, are means, not ends in themselves. Like Hume, he understood that it is no easy matter to determine which institutions best promote civilized values. Nearly everything depends on history and circumstances. This is a truth forgotten by the late twentieth-century cult of democratic capitalism.

VOLTAIRE'S POSTERITY

It is difficult to mark the limits of superstition.
Voltaire[20]

Since Voltaire wrote, much of Europe has become largely post-Christian. Both the authority of the Christian churches and the influence of Christian belief have become marginal. In Britain today, practising Christians are only one among several cultural minorities. At the same time, with the dwindling of Christian belief and practice, secularism has disappeared as a militant movement from nearly all European countries. Like a Victorian monument, standing windswept and unvisited in an empty town square, atheism has become a memorial to a battle that most people have forgotten. In so far as it was a campaign against Christianity, Voltaire's philosophy – like his tragic plays and heroic verses – has dated beyond recovery.

It is not so much that Christianity has been abandoned in favour of atheism. Rather, the concepts and categories in which atheists and Christians disputed have fallen into disuse and unintelligibility. No doubt in some countries its influence lives on in anomalous disputes about abortion, euthanasia, sexuality and similar matters. But Christianity is no longer the worldview that animates any contemporary European country.

The Enlightenment successor faith that Voltaire propagated has entered the bloodstream of all European cultures. We are all Voltaire's posterity. If it was ever possible to roll back the Enlightenment in European life, as its enemies from J.G. Hamann, J.-J. Rousseau and Joseph de Maistre through the Nazis and some thinkers of the Frankfurt School hoped, it is so no longer. Enlightenment thinking has become an integral part of our identities. We cannot deny the Enlightenment without rejecting ourselves.

We have no traditions that have not been partly shaped by Enlightenment ideals. In political life, all parties offer variations on the same Enlightenment project. By so doing they show how far the Enlightenment has come in shaping modernity in Europe. Indeed, given the ubiquity of Enlightenment thinking in modern Europe, it may well seem that Voltaire's core project – dislodging Christianity as the foundation of European life and replacing it with his Enlightenment creed of humanity – has succeeded.

Yet, as Christianity has waned in European countries as a living faith, so has the Enlightenment. Though it has succeeded in dominating modern thought, there is much in late modern European life that the Enlightenment failed to anticipate. The decline of Christianity has not gone with mass acceptance of any Enlightenment worldview. Late modern European societies such as Britain are surely post-Christian; but they are also largely post-secular. Along with other *philosophes*, Voltaire exaggerated greatly the rupture in European cultural traditions that the Enlightenment exemplified. It did not occur to him that the Enlightenment might prove to be an incident in the decline of Christianity.

The retreat of traditional religion has not been followed by an advance in rationality. The prestige of science has turned out to be no hindrance to magical thinking. Late modern societies abound in occult and millenarian cults. They are full of short-lived New Age religions, 'flickering and fading', as J.G. Ballard has put it, 'like off-peak commercials'. Voltaire's hopes of a modern natural religion were entirely in vain. Nowhere has his rational, deistic religion taken hold. If the history of late modern Europe is any guide, Voltaire's Enlightenment identification of modernity with secularism is groundless and indeed unreasonable.

Beyond Europe the spread of modernity has diverged still further from the expectations of Enlightenment thinkers. In many countries modernization has been fuelled by rejection of western, Enlightenment ideologies. In post-communist Russia, in neo-communist China, in Turkey, in India, Malaysia, Singapore and Japan, the Enlightenment is only one strand in late modernity, and not always the strongest. In the United States, where the Enlightenment project of a universal civilization is at its most militant, fundamentalist movements are more powerful than in any European country.

Twentieth-century history does not support Voltaire's expectations of how modernity was bound to develop. It is not only that science and technology have been deployed in the service of war and tyranny. That would hardly have surprised Voltaire. It is not even that the growth of human knowledge has enabled unprecedented crimes against humanity such as the Holocaust to be committed. It is that there is no detectable connection between the adoption of new technologies or the emergence of science-based economies and the spread of a universal civilization of the kind the *philosophes* imagined.

The Islamist commander directing military operations from his cellular telephone is a familiar late twentieth-century figure. The rulers of China support economic modernization; but not in order that China can be incorporated into a universal civilization. They seek to assure the survival and independence of Chinese culture. Many other examples could be cited.

There appears to be no systematic, enduring link between the adoption of modern technology and science and acceptance of an Enlightenment worldview or values. To be sure, Old Believers in Enlightenment will insist that, later or sooner, modernity and Enlightenment will prove to be one and the same. But that is not a conclusion of dispassionate inquiry on their part. It is a confession of faith. It is a wager on the future no more dictated by reason or evidence than Pascal's famously ill-placed bet.[21]

If there are those who cling to the Enlightenment today, it is not from conviction. It is from fear of what will become of them if they give it up. In truth we can neither abandon the Enlightenment nor preserve it. Its successes prevent our returning to the (perhaps imaginary) traditional forms of life defended by thinkers of the European Counter-Enlightenment. No modern society that has tasted the fruits of science and history can suppress the knowledge that it has thereby gained.

Yet these achievements of the Enlightenment have undermined it. A better knowledge of history and anthropology of the kind the Enlightenment propagated has disclosed a variety of human cultures greater than any the *philosophes* dreamt of. It is harder now than it was in Voltaire's day to specify the core values of civilization – if that term retains any meaning. The critical habit of mind inculcated in Enlightenment cultures has in our time worked to relativize values – including those of the Enlightenment. Perhaps it is only fitting that the Enlightenment (like Christianity) should perish of the virtues it had itself inculcated in us.

When he identified the Enlightenment with modernity, Voltaire was expressing a hope that turned out to be groundless. When Enlightenment thinkers affirm the same identity today, they are propagating a mere superstition. Voltaire's thought is narrow and time-bound in many ways. Yet it remains a powerful corrective of Enlightenment illusions. Enlightenment thinking in our time is animated by moral hopes far more delusive and unreasonable than the eighteenth-century optimisms that Voltaire mocked. It is difficult to know what sustains these hopes. It cannot be the history of the twentieth century – the worst in human history, as Isaiah Berlin described it.

It may be that the disenchantment of the world that the Enlightenment has achieved can be tolerated by cultures that were once Christian only when it is masked by moral hopes inherited from Christianity. Without the irrational faith that reason will someday bring harmony to the rivalry of goods and evils, human history must seem a tale told by an idiot.

When the habits of critical thought we have learnt from the Enlightenment are applied to the hopes of the Enlightenment, they prove to be exaggerated, insubstantial or illusive. The findings of science do not support the hopes of Enlightenment humanism. A Darwinian view of humanity shows it to be a species from which the capacities of

51

rational thought required by an Enlightenment civilization cannot be reasonably expected. The enterprise of scientific inquiry on which the Enlightenment wagered so much suggests that the Enlightenment's humanist hopes are misplaced. Nietzsche – late modern Europe's greatest Enlightenment thinker – was not mistaken when he anticipated that the final result of the Enlightenment would be the fracturing of its own morality.

Voltaire's 'philosophy' has little to teach us. His political relativism remains an indispensable prophylactic against the doctrinaire disorders of liberal thinking. His most valuable legacy to us may be his refusal of the consolations of theodicy – including the Enlightenment theodicy that guided him throughout his life. Voltaire's ambition of helping humankind to be 'a little less miserable' may prove to be the Enlightenment's most valuable inheritance.

For us, to be successors to the Enlightenment is a historical fate. In truth, as an unintended consequence of the Enlightenment itself, the Enlightenment is already behind us. This self-undermining effect of the Enlightenment is an irony that Voltaire, for all the luminous clarity of his pessimism, could not have foreseen.

Voltaire's thought enables us to achieve a distance from the Enlightenment that its avowed enemies – in his time or ours – have never attained. By studying Voltaire, the Enlightenment thinker *par excellence*, we understand better what it means to think and live after the Enlightenment.[22]

NOTES

1. Isaiah Berlin, 'The divorce between the sciences and the humanities', in *Against the Current: Essays in the History of Ideas* (Clarendon Press, Oxford, 1991), p. 88.

2. William Blake, *Blake's Poetry and Designs*, ed. M.L. Johnson and J.E. Grant (W.W. Norton, New York and London, 1979), p. 184.

3. Voltaire, *Philosophical Dictionary* (J. and H T Hunt, London, 1824), vol. VI, 'Singing', p. 102.

4. Peter Reading, *Last Poems* (Chatto and Windus, London, 1994), 'Fates of Men', p. 10.

5. Voltaire, *Candide and Other Stories*, new translation by Roger Pearson (Oxford University Press, Oxford, World's Classics, 1990), p. 151.

6. Voltaire, *Philosophical Dictionary*, op. cit., vol. I, 'Atheism', p. 328.

7. See Carl L. Becker, *The Heavenly City of the Eighteenth Century Philosophers* (Yale University Press, New Haven and London, 1963). For critical comment on Becker's interpretation of the Enlightenment, see Raymond O. Rockwood (ed.), *Carl Becker's Heavenly City Revisited* (Archon Books, 1968).

8. Voltaire, *Candide and Other Stories*, op. cit., pp. 8, 10.

9. Voltaire, *Philosophical Dictionary*, op. cit., vol. III, 'Good', p. 352.

10. Ludwig Wittgenstein, *Bemerkungen über Frazer's Golden Bough*, ed. Rush Rhees (Brynmill Press, Doncaster, 1979).

11. Blaise Pascal, *Pensées* (Penguin, Harmondsworth, 1966), no. 126.

12. Voltaire, *Correspondence*, ed. Theodore Besterman, 107 vols (Geneva, 1953–65), vol. LXVI, 4 June 1767.

13. Voltaire, *Notebooks*, ed. Theodore Besterman, 2 vols (Geneva, 1952) continuous pagination, p. 313.

14. 'My early beliefs', in John Maynard Keynes, *Essays and Sketches in Biography* (Meridian, New York, 1956), p. 253.

15. Voltaire, *Philosophical Dictionary*, op. cit., vol. VI, 'Toleration', p. 272.

16. See T.E. Hulme, *Speculations: Essays on Humanism and the Philosophy of Art* (Routledge and Kegan Paul, London, 1924) and *Further Speculations* (University of Nebraska, Press, Lincoln, Nebraska, 1955).

17. Friedrich Nietzsche, *The Will to Power* (Vintage, New York, 1968), pp. 62, 63, 64.

18. Voltaire, *Political Writings*, ed. David Williams (Cambridge University Press, Cambridge, 1994), 'The ABC: Seventh Conversation: That modern Europe is better than Ancient Europe', p. 131.

19. On de Sade, see Geoffrey Gorer, *The Life and Ideas of the Marquis de Sade* (Peter Owen, London, 1934).

20. Voltaire, *Philosophical Dictionary*, op. cit., vol. VI, 'Superstition', p. 219.

21. I have elsewhere argued that Enlightenment expectations of modernity have been falsified. See my book, *Enlightenment's Wake: Politics and Culture at the Close of the Modern Age* (Routledge, London, 1995).

22. I am grateful to Prof. John Burrow and Dr G. W. Smith for illuminating comments on the first draft of this book. Any remaining errors are mine.